Helping Children See Jesus

ISBN: 978-1-64104-046-4

THE CRUCIFIXION PART 1
The Road to the Cross
New Testament Volume 11: Life of Christ Part 11

Author: Ruth B. Greiner
Illustrator: Frances H. Hertzler
Computer Graphic Artist: Ed Olson
Typesetting and Layout: Morgan Melton, Patricia Pope

© 2018 Bible Visuals International
PO Box 153, Akron, PA 17501-0153
Phone: (717) 859-1131
www.biblevisuals.org

All rights reserved. No part of this publication may be reproduced, stored in a retrieval system or transmitted in any form by any means, electronic, mechanical, photocopy, recording or otherwise, without the prior permission of the publisher, except as provided by USA copyright law.

RELATED ITEMS

To access related items (such as activities, memory verse posters and translated texts) please visit our web store at shop.biblevisuals.org and enter 1011 in the search box on the page.

FREE TEXT DOWNLOAD

To access a FREE printable copy of the teaching text (PDF format) in English or other available languages, enter S1011DL in the search box. Add the item to your cart, and use coupon code XTACSV17 at checkout. Once your order is processed you will receive an email with a link to the free download.

For even the Son of Man came not to be ministered unto, but to minister, and to give His life a ransom for many.

Mark 10:45

© Bible Visuals International Inc

Lesson 1
THE ENTRY INTO JERUSALEM

> **NOTE TO THE TEACHER**
>
> It is interesting to observe that about one-third of all that is recorded in the first four books of the New Testament has to do with the events surrounding the death of Christ. While we cannot completely cover all the details, we shall use this volume and the next to try to be as thorough as possible.
>
> One of the fascinating studies of Scripture is fulfilled prophecy. Many of the details up to and including the death of Christ were clearly foretold in the Old Testament. We shall see how some of those prophecies were fulfilled.
>
> In this lesson we see a prophecy fulfilled when Jesus entered into Jerusalem riding on a donkey colt. Although Jesus offered Himself as King of Israel that day, He was rejected. Because He had known His people would reject Him, He told them they would be punished. Their beautiful capital city (Jerusalem), He said, would be completely destroyed. (See Luke 19:43-44.) And it was! (Titus and his Roman army destroyed it in the year AD 70.)
>
> As Jerusalem was punished for rejecting Him, so there is punishment for the sinner who rejects Him: eternal separation from God.

Scripture to be studied: Matthew 21:1-17; Mark 11:1-11; Luke 19:28-44; John 12:12-19; Psalm 118:26; Zechariah 9:9.

The *aim* of the lesson: Seek to lead your students to understand that the Lord Jesus Christ waits for each individual to recognize and receive Him as Saviour and King.

What your students should *know*: Someday the Lord Jesus will return to earth and reign as King. Until then He desires to rule the heart of each believer.

What your students should *feel*: A desire to let the Lord Jesus Christ rule their hearts and minds.

What your students should *do*: Give the Lord Jesus the right to control their lives.

Lesson outline (for the teacher's and students' notebooks):

1. Jesus prepares to enter Jerusalem (Matthew 21:1-6; Mark 11:1-6; Luke 19:28-34).
2. Crowds of people praise Jesus (Matthew 21:7-9; Mark 11:7-10; Luke 19:35-40; John 12:12-19).
3. Jesus weeps over Jerusalem (Luke 19:41-44; Matthew 21:10-11).
4. Jesus rebukes the Jewish leaders (Matthew 21:12-17; Mark 11:11).

The verse to be memorized:

For even the Son of man came not to be ministered unto, but to minister, and to give His life a ransom for many. (Mark 10:45)

THE LESSON

For hundreds of years the people of Israel (known as Israelites or Jews) had been waiting for One to come from God–One who would be their King. God had caused the prophet Isaiah to predict that the coming One would sit upon the throne and rule the kingdom of Israel. (See Isaiah 9:6-7.) God had the Psalmist write another prophecy about the One who would come: "He will have dominion also from sea to sea . . . Yea, all kings will fall down before Him; all nations will serve Him" (Psalm 72:8, 11).

The Jewish people knew that God would keep His promise. What they did not grasp was that before the promised One would rule His Kingdom, He had to suffer and die as a sacrifice for the sins of all people everywhere. It seems strange they did not understand this, for that He should suffer was foretold as clearly as the fact that He would be King. In the next volume of lessons we shall learn some of the Scriptures that prophesied His suffering. (*Teacher*: You may want to discuss briefly two of these prophecies: Psalm 22:1-21; Isaiah 53:7-9.)

Because God has all knowledge, He knew exactly how the Jewish people would respond to the Lord Jesus when He offered Himself to be their King. Here is what happened:

1. JESUS PREPARES TO ENTER JERUSALEM
Matthew 21:1-6; Mark 11:1-6; Luke 19:28-34

The Lord Jesus and His disciples left the town of Bethany where they had been visiting. They walked along the road that led over the Mount of Olives to Jerusalem. When they reached a small town (Bethphage) on the mountain slope, Jesus said to two of His disciples, "Go into the village. As you enter you will find a donkey and a colt upon which no one has ever ridden. Untie them and bring them to Me."

The disciples wondered: *What will the people in the village say when they see us untie a donkey and a colt which do not belong to us?*

Because He knew their thoughts, Jesus said, "If anyone asks why you are untying them, simply say, 'The Lord needs them.' And they will let you take them."

The two disciples may have had questions: Why does Jesus want a donkey? He has always walked before. Why does He want to ride now? But they immediately obeyed the command of the Lord Jesus.

At the crossroads, one of the disciples exclaimed, "There are the donkey and the colt tied at that house just as Jesus said!" They hurried to untie the animals.

Show Illustration #1

"Why are you untying them?" the men standing nearby demanded.

"The Lord needs them," one disciple answered.

Surprisingly the men let the disciples take the donkey and colt–as Jesus had said they would! Then the disciples realized what was about to happen. The Lord Jesus was going to ride into Jerusalem, as kings (of Israel) had done in days gone by. He would not ride elegantly (as kings usually did) on a white horse. He chose to ride simply on a donkey colt, a beast of burden. (*Teacher:* You may wish to explain that because horses were used in war, a horse would have caused the people to think of war. Donkeys were used for peaceful journeys–so the donkey colt would help them to think of peace.)

2. CROWDS OF PEOPLE PRAISE JESUS
Matthew 21:7-9; Mark 11:7-10; Luke 19:35-40; John 12:12-19

Show Illustration #2

After the disciples placed their outer robes on the colt, Jesus sat upon it. Strangely enough the colt did not kick or balk as colts ordinarily do when being ridden for the first time. Instead, that colt yielded to the control of its Creator (see John 1:3; Colossians 1:16) and willingly carried Him–the Son of God–upon its back. The disciples did not understand all that was happening. (See John 12:16.) But later they remembered that this very occasion had been foretold by the prophet Zechariah about 500 years before: "Tell Jerusalem, your King is coming to you riding humbly upon the colt of a donkey" (Zechariah 9:9).

Crowds of people gathered. Many wanted to honor Jesus. Some put their robes on the road. They cut down branches of trees and spread them as a royal carpet for Him. Others waved palms in the air.

Some walked joyfully in front of Jesus; others followed. They exclaimed: "Blessed is the King who comes in the name of the Lord! Peace in Heaven and glory in the highest! Hosanna [save now]!" Men, women and children shouted joyously for all the mighty works they had seen Jesus do–especially for having brought a dead man back to life. (See John 12:17-18.) What other king could do this? Again and again they exclaimed: "Blessed is the King who comes in the name of the Lord!"

Some of the Jewish religious leaders (the Pharisees) disliked what they heard and saw. "Master, rebuke Your followers for saying such things!" they commanded Jesus.

But Jesus answered. "I tell you that if these people would stop shouting, the stones would cry out." The Pharisees had never heard stones talk, but by now they should have known that Jesus could do anything. However, the stones did not cry out because the people kept calling out loudly.

3. JESUS WEEPS OVER JERUSALEM
Luke 19:41-44; Matthew 21:10-11

Show Illustration #3

When the procession reached the top of the Mount of Olives, the people could see before them the magnificent city of Jerusalem. Jerusalem, with its beautiful marble, stone, silver and choice wood, was regarded as one of the wonders of the world. The golden roof of the temple glittered in the sunlight. What a sight! But Jesus was not glad when He saw Jerusalem. No! Tears rolled down His cheeks even though the people around Him joyfully shouted His praises. Why did Jesus weep? Because He knew that many people in Jerusalem hated Him. They did not want Him to be their King. They would soon reject Him. Because of their rejection, God the Father would punish that city.

Looking at Jerusalem, Jesus cried, "If only you knew the peace which could be yours! But you've turned it down." He then made this prophecy: "The day [of punishment] is coming when your enemies will come upon you to destroy your city. They will not leave one stone upon another. You and your children will be punished because you rejected the opportunity God has given you" (the opportunity of receiving their King, God the Son–John 1:11).

The people waving the palm branches did not feel the sadness Jesus felt. They did not understand that their beautiful city would be destroyed. Nor did they understand that within only a few days the Lord Jesus would suffer and die, bearing upon Himself the sins of the people in Jerusalem–and the sins of all the world. So the shouting continued, "Hosanna! Blessed is He who comes in the name of the Lord, even the King of Israel."

The crowd pushed up and into Jerusalem, causing all the city to be stirred. "Who is this?" the city people demanded.

The multitude with Christ answered, "It is Jesus, the prophet from Nazareth of Galilee."

Moments before they had declared He was King. Now they called Him a prophet. They did not believe their own words! No, they did not truly accept Him as King–they believed Him to be only one more prophet. He was rejected by His own people.

4. JESUS REBUKES THE JEWISH LEADERS
Matthew 21:12-17; Mark 11:11

The Lord Jesus went to the temple. To Him, that temple was His Father's house. More and more people followed Him. The blind and lame found their way to Him and He healed them!

Show Illustration #4

More loudly than ever the children called out, "Hosanna to the Son of David!"

When the chief priests and other Jewish leaders saw the wonderful things Jesus did and when they heard the words of the children, they were angry. "Do you hear what they are saying?" they asked Jesus.

He answered, "Have you never read [in Psalm 8:2] that God brings praise out of the mouths of children?" What could the leaders say to that? Nothing!

Finally, when evening came, the Lord Jesus left the temple and returned to Bethany with His 12 disciples. What a day it had been! And, oh, what was ahead!

Some of that same crowd would shout again within a few days. But as we shall see in a later lesson, they would shout much differently.

The day of which we have studied is known in some parts of the world as Palm Sunday. The events of that day took place almost 2,000 years ago. The prophecy which said One would ride into the city of Jerusalem on a donkey colt (Zechariah 9:9) was perfectly fulfilled.

The prophecy Jesus made regarding the destruction of the city of Jerusalem was fulfilled later. For in the year AD 70, Titus and his Roman army ruined it so completely that not one stone was left upon another.

What about the prophecies which said Jesus would be King? When were they fulfilled? They were not fulfilled. Why? Because not every prophecy in the Bible has been fulfilled. And this is one of those. The day is even yet in the future when the Lord Jesus Christ will be King over the world. One day He will come from Heaven, sitting upon a white horse. On His head will be many crowns. Then He will be owned by the Jews as King. (See Revelation 19:11-16.)

Just as other prophecies have been fulfilled, this too will be fulfilled. Much more must happen before that day. We shall be studying about those events in the months ahead.

Christ came to earth the first time to be the Saviour of the world. He accomplished that purpose when He died on the cross. Today those who believe Him to be the Son of God and place their trust in Him, receive new natures. And as the donkey colt was tamed by its Creator, so the heart of a true believer is tamed by Him. (See 2 Corinthians 5:17.)

Even though we must wait for the day when He will return to earth and reign as King, today we who trust in Him may allow Him to rule our hearts and minds. Will *you* give Him that privilege?

Lesson 2
JUDAS, THE BETRAYER

Scripture to be studied: Matthew 26:1-29; Mark 14:1-26; Luke 22:1-18; John 12:1-11; 13:1-35; Psalm 41:9; Zechariah 11:12-13

The *aim* of the lesson: To teach that there must be a personal commitment to Christ–a complete change of heart.

What your students should *know*: The Lord Jesus knows if they are pretending or if they really believe in Him as the Son of God.

What your students should *feel*: Impelled to believe in the Lord Jesus.

What your students should *do*: Believe Jesus is the Son of God and receive Him as Saviour.

Lesson outline (for the teacher's and students' notebooks):

1. Mary shows her love for Jesus (Matthew 26:6-13; Mark 14:3-9; John 12:1-8).
2. Judas plans to betray Jesus (Luke 22:1-6; Mark 14:10-11; Matthew 26:14-16).
3. Jesus knows what Judas plans to do (Matthew 26:17-25; Mark 14:12-21; Luke 22:7-23; John 13:1-27).
4. Judas turns away from Jesus (John 13:28-30).

The verse to be memorized:

For even the Son of Man came not to be ministered unto, but to minister, and to give His life a ransom for many. (Mark 10:45)

NOTE FOR THE TEACHER

In this lesson, we see another prophecy fulfilled. This time the fulfillment has to do with Judas and the betrayal of Jesus Christ.

The name *Judas* means "praise of God" or "confessor." But Judas did not live up to his name. He was the one disciple who chose to have no part in the Kingdom of God. He turned away from the only true sacrifice for sin. Although he had lived close to the One who is the Way, the Truth and the Life, Judas himself was lost in sin, without hope and without Christ.

Never assume that a student is saved because he has faithfully attended your class. This particular lesson should be a warning to those who think they are safe because they go to church, "say" prayers or listen to the Bible.

THE LESSON

Judas Iscariot had been a disciple of Jesus for three years. He had hoped Jesus would become an earthly King, giving him (Judas) and the other disciples high positions in His Kingdom.

When Jesus rode into Jerusalem on the colt, it seemed to Judas that his dreams would soon come true. He doubtless joined in shouting with the other disciples: "Blessed is the King who comes in the name of the Lord." (See Luke 19:37-38.)

But Jesus was not made King that day. He was not on the royal throne in Jerusalem. He did not have a golden crown upon His head. And Judas had not been made an important person in the government. Judas surely thought to himself: *What is the use of hoping any longer?*

1. MARY SHOWS HER LOVE FOR JESUS
Matthew 26:6-13; Mark 14:3-9; John 12:1-8

Then came the feast in the house of Simon the Leper at Bethany. It may have been a feast of thanksgiving. Simon, healed of his leprosy, would want to say "Thank You" to the Lord Jesus–who was present with His disciples. And Lazarus who was there, would also want to say "Thank You"–for He had just been raised from the dead! (See John 12:1.) Mary and Martha, sisters of Lazarus, were there too.

Martha served fine foods at the feast. The others talked and ate together leaning on their couches with their heads toward the table.

Show Illustration #5

Then it happened! The whole room was suddenly perfumed with a sweet scent. Mary was pouring expensive perfume on the head and feet of Jesus. Some of the disciples, led by Judas, were indignant. They would have snatched the perfume from Mary. But it was too late. She had poured it all on the Lord. Using her long hair as a towel, Mary dried the feet of Jesus. It was her way of showing she loved Him very much.

Judas could not keep quiet. "Why did she waste that expensive perfume?" he asked. "It could have been sold for a year's salary (of a rural worker) and the money given to poor people."

Judas did not care about poor people. What he really cared for was money. He wanted money for himself. Judas was the treasurer for the disciples. He kept all their money in a bag, and whenever food or clothing had to be bought, Judas paid for it from the money bag. The other disciples did not know that sometimes Judas would steal money from the bag and keep it for himself. (See John 12:6.) But Jesus knew.

Jesus turned to Judas and said, "Let her alone. Why do you trouble this woman? She has done a good thing to Me. You always have the poor with you, and whenever you want to, you can do good to them. But you will not always have Me. Mary has done what she could. She poured this perfume upon Me to prepare Me for burial."

Burial? What did Jesus mean? Was He *not* going to be King on earth after all? Was He really going to die and be buried? The hopes of Judas were gone–completely gone. He would not have a high position in the Kingdom. So he no longer wanted to be a disciple of Jesus. The sad truth was that Judas never truly believed in Jesus. (See John 6:64-71.) Yet Jesus had chosen Judas as one of His disciples. This was another fulfillment of Scripture. God had foretold it. (Read Psalm 41:9.)

2. JUDAS PLANS TO BETRAY JESUS
Luke 22:1-6; Mark 14:10-11; Matthew 26:14-16

Judas left the feast at Bethany with hatred in his heart. In fact, Satan himself entered into Judas and put into his mind a wicked plan. Judas knew that the chief priests in Jerusalem were enemies of Jesus and wanted to arrest Him. So Judas hurried, determined to help them make that arrest!

Show Illustration #6

Secretly he made his way to those enemies. Greedily he asked, "How much money will you give me if I deliver Jesus to you?"

The chief priests could hardly believe what they heard. A disciple of Jesus was actually offering to help them arrest Him! Immediately they promised to pay 30 pieces of silver (about five weeks' wages) if Judas would lead them to Jesus. Judas loved money. He was willing to betray Jesus for only 30 pieces of silver, the price paid in those days for a slave. And another prophecy was fulfilled! God had said 500 years before that this very thing would happen! (*Teacher:* Read Zechariah 11:12.)

Judas promised to let the chief priests know when they could catch Jesus.

3. JESUS KNOWS WHAT JUDAS PLANS TO DO
Matthew 26:17-25; Mark 14:12-21; Luke 22:7-23; John 13:1-27

Two days later Jesus told Peter and John, "Go prepare the Passover for us to eat." He wanted them to kill a lamb for the meal. This they would eat with unleavened bread (having no yeast).

"Where do You want us to go?" the men asked Him.

"Go into the city of Jerusalem and there you will meet a man carrying a pitcher of water. Follow him into the house where he goes and say to the man who lives there, 'The Master wants to know where the guest room is where He can eat the passover with His disciples.' He will show you a large room upstairs all ready for us. Prepare the meal there."

The two disciples went immediately and found the man carrying a pitcher. They followed him to the house: everything was exactly as Jesus said it would be! There the disciples prepared the food.

That evening Jesus and His disciples gathered around the table for the passover meal. Judas was there too. But he did not tell his wicked secret.

To the disciples Jesus said, "I have looked forward to eating this passover with you before I suffer." Judas was thinking of his own evil plan to betray the Son of God.

During the meal, Jesus stopped eating. "I have something to tell you," He said. "One of you is going to betray Me."

The disciples were shocked. Could one of them really betray the Son of God? They began to question among themselves which one it might be. Some asked Jesus, "Is it I?"

Peter motioned to John (who was sitting next to Jesus) to ask Jesus who would be the one to betray Him. John leaned close to the Lord and whispered, "Lord, who is it?"

Jesus answered, "It is the one to whom I shall give this piece of bread [sop] after I have dipped it into the dish." (A sop was a token of affection.)

Show Illustration #7

Then Jesus dipped a piece of bread into the dish and gave it to Judas. Judas! Would he receive it? Yes, he did! He should have repented and asked Jesus to forgive him for the wicked thing he was planning to do. Instead he had put himself under the absolute control of Satan. No longer was there any possibility of repentance. Judas was determined to betray the Son of God that very night.

Jesus, looking at Judas, said, "What you are going to do, do quickly."

The other disciples did not know what Jesus meant. They thought He was sending Judas on an errand to buy something or give some money to the poor. (See John 13:28-29.)

4. JUDAS TURNS AWAY FROM JESUS
John 13:28-30

Show Illustration #8

Judas got up and left the table. He turned from Jesus and went out into the night–alone.

Before this, Judas had been with God the Son for three years. He had listened to the things Jesus taught. But his sinful heart had never changed. He was a pretender. There was One, however, whom Judas could not deceive and that was Jesus Christ. Jesus knew the heart of Judas–just as He knows your heart and my heart. He knows today if you are only a pretender or if you truly trust in Him as the Son of God.

If you have never received the Lord Jesus as your Saviour, will you do so today? Then–and only then–will you be able to enjoy companionship with Him.

Lesson 3
THE SUPPER OF OUR LORD–GETHSEMANE

NOTE TO THE TEACHER

In this lesson we again see prophecy fulfilled. Zechariah 13:7 speaks of the "smiting" of our Shepherd, Jesus Christ, and the scattering of His sheep. In fulfillment, we learn that His smiting included the awful betrayal of Judas Iscariot; the loneliness as He prayed in the garden; being led away by the soldiers and deserted by all His disciples. Indeed, His sheep were scattered.

The portrayal of the Son of God as He gives Himself completely to the will of His Father is a touching scene. Jesus could have escaped from His enemies as He had done before when they tried to kill Him. But the time had come for Him to give His life a ransom for many.

May we be so constrained by the love of Christ that nothing stops *us* from doing the will of God.

Scripture to be studied: Matthew 26:26-56; Mark 14:22-50; Luke 22:19-54; John 13:31-38; 18:1-13; Zechariah 13:7

The *aim* of the lesson: To teach that Jesus Christ, the Son of God, gave Himself completely in obedience to the will of God.

What your students should *know*: The Lord Jesus let nothing hinder Him from doing the will of His Father.

What your students should *feel*: Constrained to do the will of God.

What your students should *do*: Allow the Lord Jesus to control their lives completely.

Lesson outline (for the teacher's and students' notebooks):

1. Jesus introduces a simple way to remember His death (Matthew 26:26-29; Mark 14:22-25; Luke 22:19-20; John 13:31-35).
2. Jesus prays in the garden (Matthew 26:30-39; Mark 14:26-36; Luke 22:39-44; John 18:1).
3. The disciples fall asleep instead of praying (Matthew 26:40-45; Mark 14:37-41; Luke 22:45-46).
4. Jesus is betrayed by Judas and arrested (Matthew 26:46-56; Mark 14:42-50; Luke 22:47-54; John 18:2-13).

The verse to be memorized:

For even the Son of Man came not to be ministered unto, but to minister, and to give His life a ransom for many. (Mark 10:45)

THE LESSON

1. JESUS INTRODUCES A SIMPLE WAY TO REMEMBER HIS DEATH
Matthew 26:26-29; Mark 14:22-25; Luke 22:19-20; John 13:31-35

Jesus sat with His disciples at the passover table in the upper room. He knew this was to be His last night before He would die. He knew also that Judas had gone out to betray Him to His enemies. Jesus turned to the 11 disciples who were still with Him. "My time has come," He said. "Now the glory of God will be shown. God will receive great praise because of all that will happen to Me. My dear children, I shall be with you only a little while before I must leave you. You will search for Me, but you will not be able to come where I am going. So now I give you a new commandment: 'Love one another even as I have loved you.' In this way people will know that you are My disciples."

Peter did not seem interested in the new commandment. But he was concerned that Jesus had said He was leaving them. So Peter asked, "Lord, where are You going?"

Jesus replied, "Where I am going you cannot follow Me now. But you will follow Me later." Then Jesus said something that greatly disturbed the disciples: "Tonight all of you will run away and desert Me. But after I am brought to life again, I shall go before you into Galilee."

"Run away and desert You?" Peter cried in disbelief. "No! Not I! Even if all the others run away. I shall never desert You. I shall lay down my life for You."

Jesus replied, "Peter, before the rooster crows twice tomorrow morning, you will deny Me three times. You will say you do not even know Me!"

Peter declared, "Even if I must die with You, I shall not deny You!" The others made the same promise to Jesus. Not one believed he could deny the Son of God.

Show Illustration #9

Then Jesus did something special. This was the last meal He would eat with His disciples before His death. He wanted them to have something by which they could always remember Him. He took some bread, gave thanks to God for it then broke it into pieces. Giving the pieces to the disciples, He said, "Take, eat. This is My body which is given for you. When you eat this bread, remember Me."

Jesus then took some fruit-of-the-vine juice. After thanking God for it, He gave it to the disciples. "All of you drink of it," He said. "This is My blood which is shed for many for the forgiveness of sins."

Did the disciples understand what the Lord Jesus meant by all this? It was as if He gave them a picture. Even though He had not yet died, He was saying that the bread was a symbol which represented His body. Soon His body would be given in death so sinners who place their trust in Him could have eternal life. At His death, blood would flow from the gaping wounds in His hands and feet (as the Psalmist had prophesied in Psalm 22:16). The juice, He said, was a symbol of His blood. It would be a reminder to the one who truly trusted in Him, that his sins had been forgiven. Forgiveness of sin could be had no other way, for "without the shedding of blood is no forgiveness" (Hebrews 9:22).

"Eat this bread, drink the fruit of the vine," Jesus told them, "remembering Me." And for almost 2,000 years, believers have been remembering Him in a simple service known as *Breaking of Bread, Communion, The Lord's Supper* or *The Lord's Table*

2. JESUS PRAYS IN THE GARDEN
Matthew 26:30-39; Mark 14:26-36; Luke 22:39-44; John 18:1

After the disciples had observed that simple memorial, they sang a hymn. Then they went out together to the Mount of Olives. When they crossed the Kidron brook they came to the Gethsemane garden near Jerusalem.

Jesus stopped and said to eight of His disciples, "Sit down here while I go over there to pray."

– 23 –

Show Illustration #10

Taking Peter, James and John with Him, He went farther into the garden. "I am deeply troubled," He told them. "You wait here and watch with Me while I pray."

Jesus went on alone (about as far as one could throw a stone). There He fell to the ground and prayed, "O My Father, if it is possible, let this cup pass away from Me. Yet I do not want to do My will. Your will be done."

The Lord Jesus Christ knew He was facing death. He knew that, though He had never, never sinned, He would take on Himself all the sins of the whole world (Isaiah 53:6; 1 Peter 2:24). Can you understand what this meant to Him?

Imagine, if you can, that though you had not done wrong, you were to be punished for the sins which your brother committed, the sins of your sister, the sins of every person in this town. How would you feel? (Discuss.) You cannot begin to understand what the perfect Son of God felt that long ago night. For He took on Himself the sins of all the world–the sins of every man, every woman, every boy, every girl. He–the perfect, holy Son of God–was made sin for the whole world. (See 2 Corinthians 5:21.) But the Lord Jesus did it willingly, for this was the will of His Father.

As Jesus prayed, an angel from Heaven came to strengthen Him. Jesus continued to pray–but His heart became heavier. The thought of having to become the sin-bearer was what troubled Him. So great was the burden and so earnest was He in praying that the perspiration began to drop from His forehead like great drops of blood.

3. THE DISCIPLES FALL ASLEEP INSTEAD OF PRAYING
Matthew 26:40-45; Mark 14:37-41; Luke 22:45-46

Show Illustration #11

After a while Jesus went to Peter, John and James. Had they, too, been praying? No! They were tired. So they had fallen asleep.

Jesus called, "Peter, are you sleeping? Could you not watch with Me for one hour? Watch and pray so you will not enter into temptation." But the disciples were too tired to keep their eyes open. So Jesus left them. Again, He prayed, "O My Father, if this cup cannot pass away unless I drink it, Your will be done." How bitter was the cup of suffering for the sin of the world!

Jesus returned to the disciples, but again they were asleep. So He went back and prayed the same prayer the third time.

Jesus knew the time had come when He was to drink the cup of the wrath of God against sin. And He was ready to pay the supreme sacrifice for sin.

To the sleeping disciples He said, "Sleep on, take your rest." The time to pray and watch with Him was past.

4. JESUS IS BETRAYED BY JUDAS AND ARRESTED
Matthew 26:46-56; Mark 14:42-50; Luke 22:47-54; John 18:2-13

Knowing He was about to be arrested, Jesus added, "The hour is come. The Son of man is betrayed into the hands of sinners. Get up now! Let us be going. See! Here comes the one who is going to betray Me."

Through the darkness the disciples saw rushing toward them men with lanterns, torches, swords and clubs. And Judas was leading the group! He had brought the enemies of Christ–soldiers, officers from the chief priest, scribes and Pharisees.

Jesus (though He knew what they wanted) asked, "For whom are you looking?"

"Jesus of Nazareth!" they shouted.

"I am He," Jesus said.

His enemies were so shocked at His answer that they stepped backward falling at His feet.

Again Jesus asked, "For whom are you looking?"

Once more they answered, "Jesus of Nazareth."

Show Illustration #12

"I told you I am He," Jesus said. "So since I am the one you want, let My disciples go their way." He was concerned for His disciples. He did not want them to be harmed.

"Hail, Teacher!" Judas called out. And he kissed Jesus! It was as if Judas said to the enemies, "I was with Him tonight in His inner circle. He will not resist. See? He let me kiss Him!"

No, Jesus did not draw away from Judas. He simply asked him, "Do you betray the Son of man with a kiss?"

Then the soldiers surrounded Jesus. When Peter saw what was happening, he snatched his sword from its sheath and cut off the right ear of Malchus (a servant of the high priest)–one of the men who was arresting Christ.

Jesus was not pleased. "Peter," He ordered, "put your sword away. I could call to My Father and He would even now send Me more than 12 legions [thousands, even millions!] of angels. But how then would the Scriptures be fulfilled? It must be this way." Then Jesus touched the ear of Malchus and healed him.

The soldiers seized Jesus and tied His hands, making Him a prisoner. Turning to the chief priests and captains of the temple, Jesus asked, "Have you come out with swords and clubs to take Me as you would take a robber? I sat with you daily in the temple and you did not arrest Me. But this is your hour and the power of darkness. All this is come to pass that the Scriptures of the prophets might be fulfilled."

Another prophecy fulfilled? Yes! Which one this time? Psalm 41:9: "Yes, My own familiar friend, in whom I trusted, who did eat of My bread, has lifted up his heel against Me." (See also John 13:18-19.) Judas had accepted the sop, a token of His affection. And now he had betrayed the One who loved him as no one else could ever love him.

As Jesus allowed Himself to be led away, all of His disciples–every one of them–turned and fled!

> **NOTE TO THE TEACHER**
>
> To assure that your students will never be confused by those who teach that the bread and wine is changed into the actual body and blood of the Lord Jesus Christ, you may wish to use this simple object lesson. Show them a picture of someone (your mother perhaps), explaining, "If I say to you 'This is my mother,' you are not misled. You know that this piece of heavy paper is not my mother. It is a *picture* of my mother. So when Jesus said, 'This is My body . . . this is My blood . . . ,' He was teaching that the bread and wine were symbols (pictures) of His body and His blood."
>
> Depending upon the Bible knowledge of your students, you may wish to explain more fully why the soldiers fell on the ground when Jesus revealed that He was the One for whom they were looking. It is this: Jesus used for Himself a name for the Lord God when He answered them, saying *I AM*. (See Exodus 3:6, 13-14; John 8:52-58; John 18:6.) This is a holy name–a name to be revered. It is the name that helps us remember that God always was, He always is, He always will be. As God the *Father* is I AM, so God the *Son* is I AM. Jesus is God the Son.

Lesson 4
THE CRUCIFIXION OF CHRIST–PART 1

The *aim* of the lesson: To make clear that the whole Bible speaks of Jesus Christ the Saviour.

What your students should *know:* Jesus gave His life as a ransom to pay the penalty of sin.

What your students should *feel:* A desire to have the Lord Jesus live and rule in their lives.

What your students should *do:*
  Unsaved: Believe on the Lord Jesus Christ as the Son of God and receive Him as Saviour.
  Saved: Allow the Lord Jesus Christ to reign in their lives as King–controlling their hearts, wills and natures.

Lesson outline (for the teacher's and students' notebooks):
1. Jesus Christ fulfilled prophecy (Isaiah 42:6; 6:10).
2. The Passover was a reminder of the lamb which died in place of the firstborn (Exodus 12:12-13).
3. The Lord Jesus, the Lamb of God, is the final sacrifice for sin (John 1:29; Hebrews 10:11-12).
4. Jesus Christ is the Saviour of the world (John 3:16).

The verse to be memorized:
For even the Son of Man came not to be ministered unto, but to minister, and to give His life a ransom for many. (Mark 10:45)

> **NOTE TO THE TEACHER**
>
> Are your students putting plenty of notes in their note-books? The reference of each fulfilled prophecy should certainly be there. The events leading to the death of Christ ought to be listed. This volume and the next are vitally important. Get the notes in *notebooks* and the truths in *hearts*!

THE LESSON

The Bible is the perfect and true Word of God. God the Holy Spirit moved on the hearts of men and caused them to write exactly what He wanted written. Prophecy is one proof of the accuracy of the Bible. In our first three lessons we studied some of the fulfilled prophecies written about our Lord. There are more than 300 prophecies concerning the first coming of Christ to earth. And all of those prophecies have been perfectly fulfilled! We can be certain, therefore, that all that is prophesied about the future will as certainly come true.

1. JESUS CHRIST FULFILLED PROPHECY
Isaiah 42:6; 6:10

What was the purpose of Jesus' riding into the city of Jerusalem? *(He was offering Himself as King of the Jews.)* (*Teacher:* Encourage a student to use illustrations #1 through 4 to review lesson #1. Give the class opportunity to tell what prophecy was fulfilled that day.)

Show Illustration #13a

Some of the people who joined that procession did so because they had been with the Lord Jesus when He raised a man to life. (See John 12:17-18.) They doubtless thought He must be the One promised by God, else how could He do such a miracle? But some of the Jewish religious leaders (Pharisees) who should have been well instructed in the Word of God, did not believe Him to be God the Son. Their very unbelief was a fulfillment of what the prophet Isaiah had written 700 years before: "Who hath believed our report?" (Isaiah 53:1; see also John 12:37-38.) No, the religious leaders did not believe any of the prophecy which Isaiah wrote in that 53rd chapter.

Show Illustration #13b

Among the crowd that first Palm Sunday were some Greeks who had become interested in the religion of the Jews. They asked to see Jesus and He told them that He would have to die. (*Teacher:* Read John 12:20-25 to the class.) If He were not to die, no one could be saved. He had come to the Jews. But hundreds of years before, Isaiah had prophesied that if the Jews rejected Him, He would become "a light of the Gentiles" (Isaiah 42:6). (Greeks–and others who are not Jews–are Gentiles.) When Jesus revealed to the Gentiles that He would die, another prophecy was fulfilled!

Having spoken of His death, Jesus said, "Now My soul is troubled." Troubled because He was thinking of the awfulness of taking upon Himself the sin of the world. But He added, "For this cause I came into the world–I came to die. Father, bring glory and honor to Your name."

Show Illustration #13c

And God the Father spoke from Heaven to His Son, saying, "I have already had glory and I shall have glory again." The Lord Jesus had honored His Father God during His life on earth. And God said He would again have honor. This time He would receive glory and honor through the death of His Son. (See John 12:27-33.)

To those who were confused by the voice from Heaven, Jesus explained, "When I am lifted up [on the cross], I shall draw everyone to Me."

He was going to die . . . die for the sins of everyone everywhere. Yet 700 years before, Isaiah the prophet had written that their eyes would be blind and their hearts hardened so they would not understand. (See Isaiah 6:10.) And, though He did many miracles before them, "yet they believed not on Him" (John 12:37). So Isaiah's prophecy was fulfilled!

2. THE PASSOVER WAS A REMINDER OF THE LAMB WHICH DIED IN PLACE OF THE FIRSTBORN
Exodus 12:12-13

Show Illustration #14a

Later that week our Lord ate the passover feast with His disciples. The passover was a reminder of something which had already happened. But it was also a picture of something that was going to happen.

Almost 1,500 years before the Lord Jesus lived, the Jewish people were slaves in Egypt. To get them out of the hands of the slave owners and back to their homeland (Israel), God had to punish the Egyptians. The most severe punishment was the death of all the firstborn children–a punishment the *Egyptians* could not escape. However, God promised the *Jews* they could escape if each family would do one thing: kill a lamb and put its blood on the top and sides of the door.

Show Illustration #14b

"I will pass through the land of Egypt," God said, "and I will kill all the firstborn in the land of Egypt, both of man and beast . . . And the blood shall be to you for a sign upon the houses where you are. And when I see the blood, I will PASS OVER you" (Exodus 12:12-13). And it was so. The Egyptians lost all their oldest children and animals. But not one of the Jews was killed.

Show Illustration #14c

So they would always remember that night, God told them to make a feast. They were to roast and eat the lamb which had died in place of the firstborn. Year after year they were to observe that special day. It was THE LORD'S PASSOVER. At each passover they were to explain to their children what God had done for them. So for hundreds of years the Jewish people ate the passover once each year. The Lord Jesus observed the passover with His disciples the night before His death. But the passover took on new meaning that night. And it was to be replaced with a new observance.

3. THE LORD JESUS, THE LAMB OF GOD, IS THE FINAL SACRIFICE FOR SIN
John 1:29; Hebrews 10:11-12

Show Illustration #15

At the beginning of His ministry, the Lord Jesus was proclaimed as the Lamb of God, the One who takes away the sin of the world. (See John 1:29.) Jesus knew that, like a passover lamb, He would die. But there was a great difference. In the past, many, many lambs had died, each taking the place of a sinner. The many lambs pictured Him, the real Lamb of God–the One who was the perfect Lamb of God. (See 1 Corinthians 5:7b.) He was the *final sacrifice* for sins forever (Hebrews 10:11-12). There would never again be the necessity of observing the passover. He had fulfilled the picture which had been given hundreds of years before He was born.

That night Christ Jesus the Lord replaced the passover observance with a simple supper–bread and wine. Before giving these to His disciples the Lord Jesus gave thanks to God. He knew that the broken bread was a symbol of His body which soon would die. But He thanked God for it. He knew that the wine was a symbol of His blood that was to be given as a substitute sacrifice for the sins of the world. But He thanked God for that poured-out blood.

Today, when Christian believers meet together and take part in the Lord's Supper, they remember Him, the Lamb of God who took upon Himself the sin of the world. Almost nothing is easier than eating broken bread and drinking juice from a cup. It is a simple exercise. Believing is also a simple exercise–simple enough for even a child. To become a child of God one must believe: believe that Jesus Christ is the Son of God; believe He died in place of each sinner; believe He wants to forgive the one who trusts Him and receives Him.

4. JESUS CHRIST IS THE SAVIOUR OF THE WORLD
John 3:16

Pictures and prophecies. This wonderful Book, the Bible, is full of them! Each time you read the Word of God, mark the sections that are pictures or prophecies of the Lord Jesus Christ. You will have a surprise to see that page after page tells something about Him.

Show Illustration #16

And what is the central and most important truth of the Bible? This: God the Father sent God the Son for the specific purpose of being the Saviour of the world. He gave His life a ransom for you–for your sin, for mine. But He did not stay dead. He arose. And He lives! He waits now, this moment, to live in your heart.

In a day yet future the Lord Jesus will reign upon a throne. Until then, if you are His child, it can be your joy to allow Him to reign as your

King–controlling your heart, your will, your nature. Will you let Him do so?

> **A NOTE TO THE TEACHER**
>
> Is the word ransom new to you? A "ransom" is a price of deliverance. All people are captives–captives of sin. Because they are sinners, a penalty must be paid for their sin. The sin penalty is death–and there is no escape.
>
> But wait! Suppose another pays our penalty. What then? Can we escape the death penalty? Yes! This is exactly why the Lord Jesus came to earth. He came to "minister," to serve. How best could He serve a sinner condemned to die? By giving His life in place of the sinner. That sinner, bound in his sin, can be set free if a ransom–the price of deliverance–is paid.
>
> What is the price of deliverance? Blood. Any blood? No, a thousand no's! The only blood which the true and living God will accept is the precious blood of His perfect, sinless Son. His Son willingly *gave* His blood for you and for every sinner of all time. He left Heaven so He could die for the sins of the world. When we believe Him to be the Son of God, when we receive Him as the One who paid the death penalty for our sin, He forgives our sin and gives us assurance of eternal life in Heaven. He loves *you*–and gave Himself for *you*. (See Galatians 2:20.)

www.ingramcontent.com/pod-product-compliance
Lightning Source LLC
Chambersburg PA
CBHW060805090426
42736CB00002B/167